LIFE

BEYOND

IF…..

There is life waiting beyond

If………..

By

VAIBHAV SRIVASTAV

e

DEDICATION

To my mother and father whose love and guidance shaped the life behind the pages

And

To all who have vision to see life beyond if.....

e

LUMAIRE PUBLISHERS

USA | Canada | UK | Ireland | Australia
New Zealand | India | South Africa | China | Singapore

Lumaire Publishers is an independent publishing house.

Published by Lumaire Publishrs
Indiae

ISBN 978-93-5782-671-6

Printed in India

INDEX

PART II – THE HIDDEN COST OF LIVING IN "WHAT IF…."

PART III - BREAKING THE "WHAT IF….." CYCLE

Chapter 8

Chapter 9

Chapter 10

Chapter 11

PART IV - LEFE BEYOND FEAR

Chapter 12

Chapter 13

Chapter 14

FINAL CHAPTER

Preface

This book was born from a simple but powerful question: "What if question is the only thing standing between us and the life we truly want?"

For years, I found myself trapped in cycles of doubt, overthinking, and hesitation. Like many others, I constantly asked "*what if?"—what if I fail, what if I'm not good enough, what if things go wrong.*

But over time, I realized something important: the real cost was not failure—it was inaction.

This book is for anyone who has ever felt stuck because of fear, uncertainty, or self-doubt. Through these pages, I aim to help you understand your fears, break free from limiting thought patterns, and take control of your life.You don't need to be fearless to move forward—you just need to be willing.

If this book helps you take even one step beyond fear, it has served its purpose.

Vaibhav Srivastav

INTRODUCTION

Many people spend their lives worrying about questions like, *"What if I fail? what if I lose my job? What if I go broke? What if I get cancer? What if she doesn't love me"* or *"What if I die without achieving anything?"* ***what if……….?*** list is infinite. These thoughts are common and part of being human. Thinking about failure and death can sometimes motivate people to work harder and find meaning in life. However, when these worries become constant, they can cause stress, anxiety, and sadness.

These Fears can stop people from trying new things or following their dreams. At the same time, these fear can make people feel uncertain about the future and question the purpose of life. When these fears are present, they may affect a person's confidence, happiness, and overall mental well-being.

These fears work together and influence a person's thoughts and behavior.

Often times, the only thing stands between you and the life you imagine for yourself is the question what if….

The only job of what if…..is to stop you hold you back, convince you to believe that you will not be able to do it,its too scary,too big,too risky,too bad.

Therefore, This book aims to help remove question what if? from your mind with the help of flow charts and diagrams.

This book is your awakening.
A reminder of who you really are.

Let us begin this journey — toward courage, clarity, and a life without limits.

Lets get started my friend.

How to read this book

Before you begin journey I want to share few lessons I learned while reading some of the books.

1.There no specific rules to read book, so feel free to read it in any way or order you want.

2.Skip the parts that are not relevant to you, you don't have to read a book cover to cover.

3. Highlight texts and take notes to remember more.

4.Note important quotes,statements in diary which help you in future.

5.You only need one idea that can change your life.If a book gives you only one piece of advice ,its already worth your time.

Happy reading.

PART 1

UNDERSTANDING FEAR

“ The moment you understand your fear, it

Stops controlling you.”

----Abraham Lincon

Psychology of fear

Fear is not in the situation; it is in the way the mind interprets it. if a person has a frightening experience with a dog, they may later fear all dogs. If a child develops a fear of the dark, they may grow up to feel as though someone is walking behind them when they are alone at night.

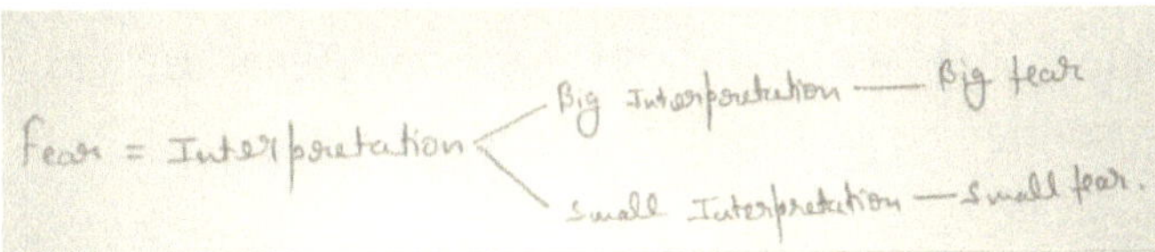

You must take responsibility—not just for your life, but also for the fears that shape it. Fear often hides deeper truths, which I will uncover in the chapters that follow.

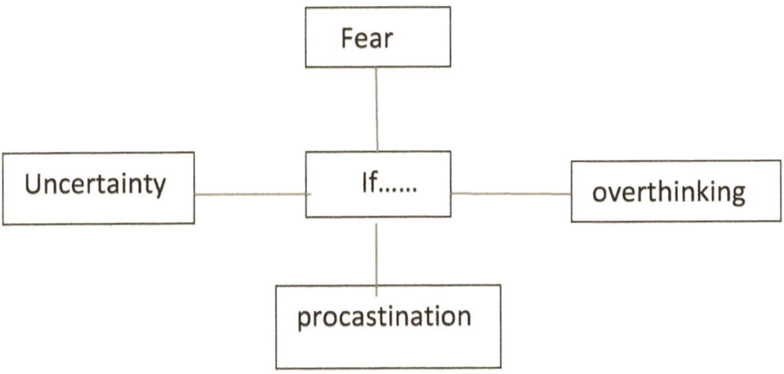

Psychological Theories of Fear

a) Classical Conditioning (Pavlov & Watson)

Fear can be learned through association. For example, if a person has a frightening experience with a dog, they may later fear all dogs.

b) Cognitive Theory

Fear depends on how we interpret a situation. If we believe something is dangerous, we feel fear — even if the threat is not real.

c) Evolutionary Theory

Fear developed to protect humans from threats like predators, heights, and darkness. Some fears are universal because they helped early humans survive.

Through these common theories, we gain a deeper understanding of fear's complexity.

- Difference between real danger vs imagined danger.

Imagined danger often feels five to ten times greater than real danger. Because

imagination has no limits.

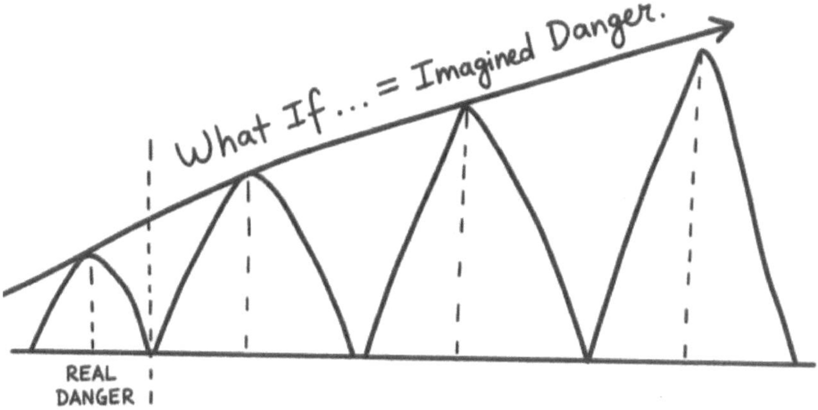

Real Danger	What If (Imagined)
1.It demands action and sharpens our senses.	1. Body reacts,heart race and mind becomes Restless.
2.It protects life.	2. It disturbs peace.

"Endless 'what if' questions—'What if I die?' 'What if I fail?'—can arise in the mind. These questions can take countless forms, and it is impossible to cover them all. Here, we will focus only on a few of the most important aspects.

"These are situations you might encounter later in life, or may have already experienced in the past. which we will discuss in the next chapter.

Is this fear protecting me from real harm, or holding me back from growth??

What "IF I die" = fear of death

simple yet powerful question: *"What if I die?"* This thought can arise suddenly—in moments of illness, uncertainty, danger, or even silence. Close your eyes for a moment and return to the last time you asked yourself, 'What would happen if I died?' Rather than fearing the question, examine it.

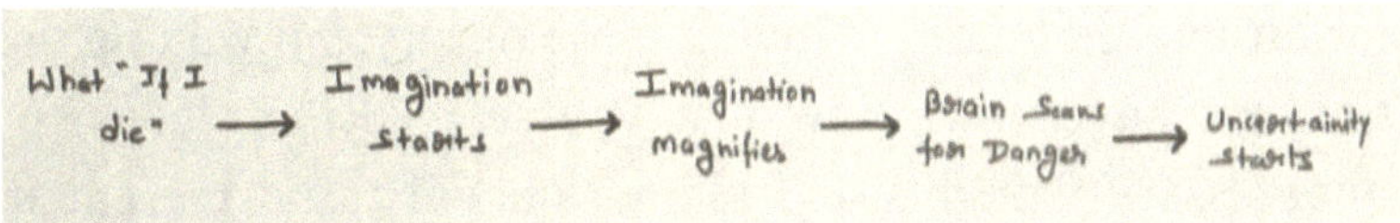

A person feels sudden chest pain or severe headache. Even before a doctor confirms anything, the mind jumps to: *"What if this is serious? What if I die?"* In reality, it may be minor—but imagination magnifies the fear.

When we hear about a sudden accident or unexpected death, we begin to reflect:
"If it happened to them, what if it happens to me?"
The mind connects another person's story to our own life.

That's common psychology of mind.

➢ What if…I loose loved ones

The fear of losing a loved one is rooted in love itself. When someone becomes our source of comfort, safety, and happiness, the idea of life without them feels unbearable. This fear often whispers "*what if*" in quiet moments,

creating anxiety about a future that has not yet arrived. But instead of letting fear steal today's joy, we can choose to turn it into gratitude — loving more deeply,and valuing the time we have now. Now that you've read this, let go of unnecessary thoughts and allow yourself to be present in this moment.

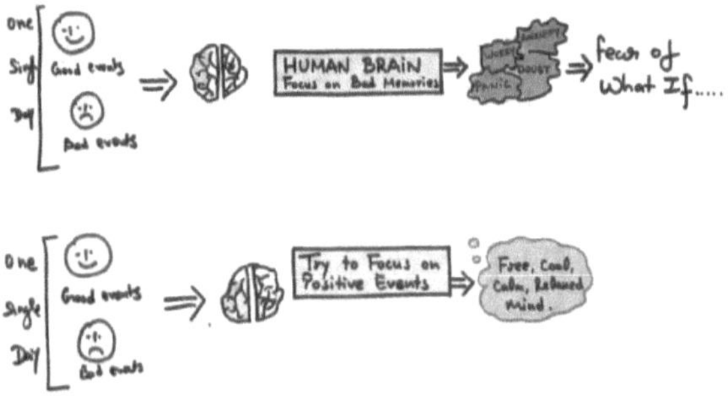

Every day, we meet countless people—sometimes knowingly, sometimes by chance—and even brief encounters leave traces in our minds. As humans, our brains have a natural habit of holding onto negative thoughts, often turning them into endless, unnecessary worries. But we have the power to train our minds to notice the positive instead. By consciously focusing on uplifting moments and experiences, we can quiet the noise, let go of unnecessary stress, and nurture a calm, relaxed mind.

- *If I focus on fear of loss, am I missing the joy of presence today?*
- *What can I do right now to show love instead of worrying about tomorrow?*

What if I fail = fear of failure

A relationship?

Something your family expects?

Something you expect from yourself?

Fear is defined differently by each individual. It largely depends on the extent of loss a person has experienced, whether mental or physical, throughout their life.

Take a deep breath and think about what "failure" really means to you.
Hold onto that definition.Now compare it with the points below.

Nothing is above my will

"This is just a chapter, not the whole story."

"One failure doesn't define my future."

"I survived 100% of my worst days so far."

"I am stronger than this moment."

"Keep going — your future self is watching."

Failure = new beginning

Daily ask yourself by repeating your name if iam unable to do such a easy things….

Now ask yourself , honestly:Is this truly a problem — or just a moment of growth in disguise

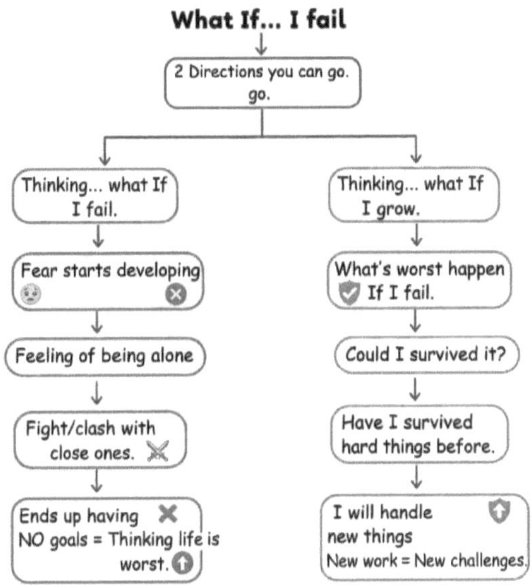

➤ Reframing failure as feedback

Failure is not a stop sign — it is a direction sign. **It tells us what to adjust, what to strengthen, and what to try differently**. When we reframe failure as feedback, we remove fear and replace it with curiosity. Instead of feeling defeated, we become determined. Every successful person

has failed — but what made them succeed was their willingness to learn from it.

Let's understand this with few stories.

1. J.K. Rowling's first *Harry Potter* book was rejected 12 times. Instead of giving up, she saw the rejections as feedback to improve her manuscript. Finally, a publisher accepted it, and today her books are loved worldwide.

accepted it, and today her books are loved worldwide. Her story shows that failure is not the end — it is a lesson guiding us toward success.

2. When Thomas Edison was trying to invent the light bulb, he failed many times. In fact, he tested thousands of different materials that did not work. Many people thought he should stop trying. But Edison did not see those attempts as failures. He said,
"I have not failed. I've just found 10,000 ways that won't work."

Each failed experiment gave him feedback. It showed him what material was not suitable. Instead of feeling discouraged, he used that information to try something different.

Finally, after many attempts, he successfully invented a working light bulb.

Edison's story teaches us that failure is not the end. It is information. When we treat failure as feedback.

Failure=bundle of mistakes=feedback=success

These are not just stories but life lessons for us even today. If you think your failure is the last step in life, read the book further.

Welcome to a world of clarity and mind refreshment with me. I hope that by now, you've enjoyed reading and perhaps discovered something that could change your daily life. If not, don't worry—hold my hand, and let's continue this journey together, as lovable companions.

Fear of rejection and judgement

The fear of rejection and judgment is one of the most deeply rooted psychological barriers individuals face, often shaping decisions, limiting potential, and influencing self-perception. It stems from a fundamental human need for acceptance and belonging, yet it can manifest as hesitation, self-doubt, or avoidance of opportunities that involve vulnerability. This fear is frequently amplified by past experiences, societal expectations, and internalized criticism, creating a cycle where individuals preemptively reject themselves to avoid external disapproval. Over time, it can restrict personal growth, creativity, and authentic expression. However, when examined closely, rejection is not a definitive measure of worth but a subjective response shaped by circumstances and perspectives. Understanding this distinction allows individuals to reframe judgment as feedback rather than condemnation, ultimately transforming fear into a catalyst for resilience, confidence, and meaningful self-development.

➢ Social media and comparison

In the digital age, social media has become a powerful catalyst for comparison, often intensifying feelings of inadequacy and self-doubt. Constant exposure to carefully curated highlights of others' lives can create an illusion of perfection, leading individuals to measure their own worth against unrealistic standards. This comparison is rarely balanced, as it overlooks the unseen struggles, failures, and complexities behind the scenes. Over time, this pattern can erode self-esteem, foster anxiety, and distort one's sense of identity and achievement. The pressure to seek validation through likes, comments, and external approval further reinforces this cycle, making self-worth increasingly dependent on public perception. Recognizing the curated nature of online content and cultivating self-awareness allows individuals to break free from this comparison trap, shifting focus from external validation to personal growth, authenticity, and inner fulfillment.

What if a single moment of comparison could quietly change how we see ourselves? Imagine scrolling through social media and seeing a friend post a photo celebrating a new job. In that instant, you feel behind, questioning your own progress. But what if that post is just one chapter of their story—one that doesn't show the rejections, uncertainty, or struggles they faced? What if, instead of comparing, you paused and reminded yourself that your journey is unfolding in its own time? In that small shift of thought, comparison loses its weight, and self-worth returns to where it belongs—within, not online.

Short-form videos, such as reels, can significantly impact emotional regulation and cognitive balance. Each reel presents a distinct emotional stimulus, and when an individual consumes a large number—sometimes hundreds per day—it results in the rapid creation of numerous emotional "scenes" in the brain.

The brain must continuously process and adjust to these shifting stimuli. For example, an emotionally intense reel may evoke sadness or empathy, immediately followed by humorous content that triggers laughter. This rapid alternation between contrasting emotional states can create internal inconsistency and cognitive strain.

Over time, such frequent and abrupt emotional shifts may disrupt the brain's ability to maintain emotional stability, potentially leading to mental fatigue and reduced emotional resilience.

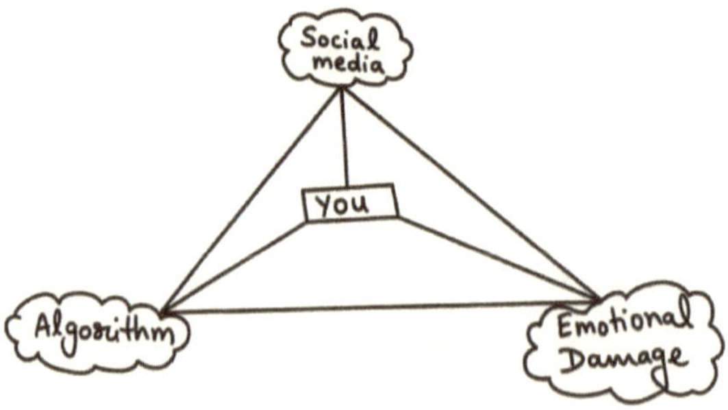

Excessive consumption of emotionally stimulating reels can contribute to mental health issues such as **Anxiety Disorder, Depression, Sleep Disorders, Attention Deficit**

Hyperactivity Disorder–like symptoms, Digital Addiction, and Emotional Burnout.

➢ Why not everyone is meant to understand you

Not everyone is meant to understand you—and that's not your failure, it's your uniqueness. You carry thoughts, feelings, and depths that come from your own journey, and not everyone has walked the same path to recognize them. Some people will misread you that won't even try, and a few will only see what they're capable of seeing—and that's okay. You were never meant to shrink yourself just to be easily understood. The right people won't need you to over-explain your heart; they'll meet you with curiosity, patience, and respect. So don't lose your voice trying to fit into someone else's understanding. Stay real, stay expressive, and trust that those who are meant to truly see you will find their way to you.

A seed has the potential to grow into something great, but only in the right soil does it flourish.

Each one carries the same truth—your depth isn't the problem; not everyone is ready or able to receive it.

- *What changes in my life when I stop seeking approval from people who don't understand me?*

- *Is my energy better spent explaining myself, or building my life?*

- Need for approval

The need for approval comes from a very human place—we all want to feel seen, accepted, and valued. But when you depend on everyone understanding or validating you, you give away control of your peace. Not everyone will get you, and that's okay. Approval from others is temporary; self-acceptance is lasting. The moment you start valuing your own voice more than outside opinions, you stop chasing validation and start living freely.

Self-worth > Others' approval = Inner peace

You share an idea or express your feelings honestly. Some people ignore it, some misunderstand it, and a few truly appreciate it.

If you depend on everyone's approval, you feel hurt and start doubting yourself.
But if you trust your own truth, you stay calm—because you know your value doesn't decrease just because others didn't recognize it.

➢ Building Internal Confidence

What if effect your confidence plays a very crucial role. ***As less the confidence more what if….*** Effect you see means more and more you starts thinking what if I fail what I will do like this all examples.

Internal confidence is not about being the loudest in the room. It is about being secure enough in yourself that you don't need to prove your worth to others.

How to built internal confidence

I will be telling you with my example as when I was new at horse riding my trainer use to hold leash of horse and he use to do walk as iam sitting on it but after some 15 days it was rainy season with big grasses on the ground he removed lunging rope and said now take him for walk. Now keep yourself in place of me then think what you will do…actually this is the chance destiny has given me to build internal confidence that yes I can and I will whatever the circumstances will be….and yes same thing happen, also I have taken that horse for walk….

By means of this example I want to tell you that life will not give big chances big reasons big tasks or big dreams,most of the time you have to see small things and build internal confidence by conquering them.by ***today only start finding opportunities in daily or day to day small works.***

PART-2

THE HIDDEN COST OF LIVING IN "WHAT IF"

"It is not the things we did in life that we regret on our deathbed, it is the things we did not."

— Randy Pausch

Dreams we never try

At every stage of life we have different dreams. but most of them not become reality due to one thinking what if……this will happen that will happen, not just now only think few days or months or year, which dream you have sacrificed for one question what if….. this happens that happens.

Regret can last a lifetime. Imagine looking back years later and wondering, "What if I had tried?" Failure may hurt for a moment, but regret can stay forever. When we attempt something, we either succeed or learn. Both outcomes help us grow. But when we never try, we gain nothing except doubt. You can count things which you have left for any reason of only question what if.

Dreams do not demand perfection; they demand effort. Taking one small step is often enough to begin. It may not lead to immediate success, but it builds confidence and experience. Courage is not the absence of fear — it is moving forward despite fear

In the end, the only dream guaranteed to fail is the one we never try. Life is too short to be lived with unanswered "what ifs." It is better to fall while chasing a dream than to stand still with regret. The future belongs to those who dare to try and overcome and face the question what iffffffff……….

Now understand it with chart.

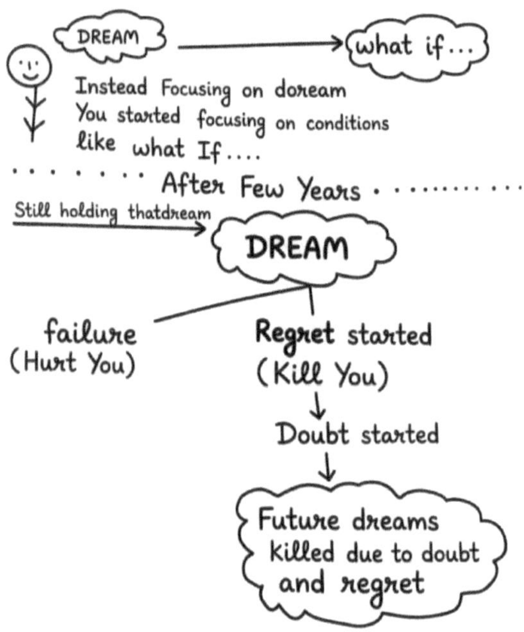

Don't spoil your future for just what if...

➢ Opportunities missed

Do not wait for big opportunities to appear. Instead, focus on the small opportunities that arise in your daily life. Have faith in yourself and move forward by making the most of these small chances. When you consistently take advantage of smaller opportunities, you gradually move closer to your larger goals — often without even realizing it. Many people spend their time searching for one big breakthrough and, in the process, ignore the valuable opportunities right in front of them. However, great achievements are rarely the result of a single moment. They are built step by step, just like grand palaces are constructed brick by brick at a time. Therefore, never underestimate or overlook small opportunities. They are the foundation that leads you toward your dreams. Sachin Tendulkar did not become a cricket legend overnight. As a young boy, he practiced for hours every single day. He played small matches, school tournaments, and local games. These were small opportunities. If he had ignored those small chances to play and improve, he would not have become one of the greatest cricketers in the world. Every small match helped him grow, and step by step, those small opportunities took him closer to his big dream. Close your eyes and now start thinking about your dream, and have a clear image about your dream…and now say I can achieve it, and slowly slowly you will have a clear idea to grab which opportunity and what to leave…but this will only help you when you will not change your dream every month or in a days means be consistent and have clear image about your dream. This idea can be best understood through the example of a sportsperson. Why can't everyone follow the same approach? For instance, Sachin Tendulkar, one of India's greatest cricketers, decided early on that he wanted to pursue a career in cricket. Once he made that decision, he actively sought out opportunities that aligned with his dream and passion. Similarly, when individuals clearly define their goals, they can begin identifying and pursuing opportunities that support their aspirations.

Once you develop the ability to understand and interpret the events occurring in your life, it becomes much easier to navigate challenges and move closer to your dreams. However, this clarity and direction are only possible when you have a focused and clear mindset.

➢ Dreams postponed

Dreams give meaning and direction to our lives. They inspire us to work hard and imagine a better future. However, sometimes dreams are not destroyed — they are postponed. A postponed dream is one that we delay because of fear, responsibilities, lack of resources, or unexpected life situations.

Have a clear vision about your dream. due to any circumstance if you want to postpone dream let it be last option. Dreams postponed should not become dreams abandoned because *A dream postponed for too long can slowly lose its energy.* Doubt replaces passion. Fear replaces confidence. People start believing that it is "too late" to begin. But the truth is, a dream has no expiry date.

Many people postpone their dreams thinking there will always be "the right time." A student may delay starting a business to focus on studies. A talented singer may choose a stable job to support family needs. A person may postpone learning a new skill because they feel they are too busy. In such cases, dreams are not forgotten, but they are pushed aside.

Promise yourself in any condition or in any circumstance I have to live my dream because once you attached yourself in, what if…..loop you will be in other zone.

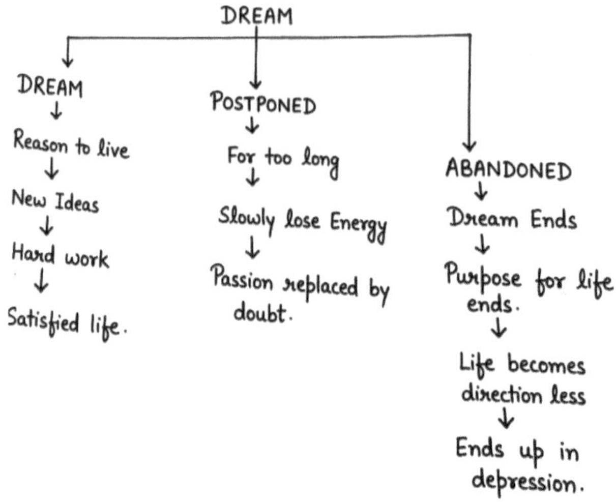

Please take a moment to carefully review this chart. Then, close your eyes and reflect on your dream once again. Consider the three categories presented and evaluate which category your dream currently falls into.

➢ The silent regret of "I wish I had tried"

One of the deepest regrets in life is the silent whisper of *"I wish I had tried."* It is not failure that weighs us down the most, but the opportunities we never pursued and the chances we were too afraid to take. Failure teaches lessons, builds resilience, and shapes growth—but regret lingers quietly, often for years. Taking a step toward your dream, no matter how small, is always better than living with the question of what might have been. Act today, so your future self feels pride instead of regret.

Some dreams can only be fulfilled when we are young, determined, and relatively free from major responsibilities. As life progresses, responsibilities increase, and time becomes limited. Therefore, certain passions are best pursued when we have the energy, courage, and freedom to do so.

For example, I always had a strong desire to learn horse riding. At the age of 24, I finally fulfilled that dream using my hard-earned money as a history teacher. The course fee was $87.42 (approximately ₹8,000). It was not just about paying the fee; it was about valuing my passion enough to invest in it.

If I had postponed this dream due to financial concerns or other life issues, I might never have experienced it. ***Life does not pause for our convenience.*** As we grow older, our bodies may not have the same strength to endure the physical demands of activities like horse riding. Health conditions, family responsibilities, and other commitments can gradually limit our ability to pursue such dreams.

If I had delayed it, there might always have been a silent regret — a lingering thought of, "I wish I had tried." That experience taught me that while responsibilities are important, we should not continuously postpone the dreams that truly matter to us. Sometimes, the right time is simply the moment we decide to begin.

The illusion of control

At the deepest level, humans are wired to seek safety. Uncertainty feels threatening because it means we cannot predict or prepare for what might happen. The brain prefers a painful certainty over an unpredictable unknown. Control becomes a psychological shield — a way to reduce anxiety and create the feeling that "nothing can hurt me if I manage everything."

Control gives the illusion of stability. It creates a temporary sense of security and competence. For someone who has experienced instability, trauma, or unpredictability in the past, the need for control can become even stronger — it feels like survival.

So the core is not dominance.
It is not arrogance.
It is not strength.

It is **fear trying to feel safe**.

Real emotional growth begins when a person learns that safety does not come from controlling everything — it comes from trusting their ability to handle whatever happens.

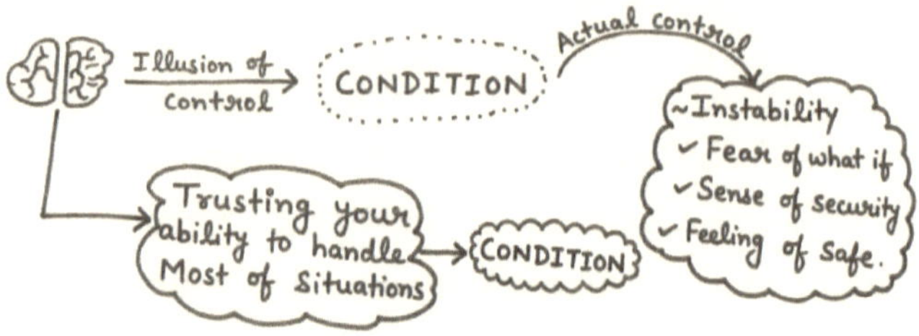

If you trust your ability to handle every situation then in real way you are can and you will handle the situation. else other than this you are only in illusion because circumstance of conditions to happen also depends on various factors like Many events in life are influenced by chance, complexity, timing, and other people's choices.

If you truly trust your ability to handle any situation, then you are more likely to manage it successfully. Confidence helps you stay calm, think clearly, and take the right actions. However, confidence alone is not enough. Many situations are influenced by factors beyond your control, such as timing, chance, complex circumstances, and the choices of other people. Believing you can handle everything without considering these factors may create a false sense of control.

Lets understand with example.

A manager micromanages every task. They don't trust employees to make decisions without approval. On the surface, it looks like they want power. Underneath? They are afraid of failure or being judged as incompetent. If everything goes through them, mistakes feel less likely. Control becomes a shield against embarrassment.The

behavior is control.
The core emotion is fear of failure.

A person constantly checks their partner's phone, asks where they are, and wants updates all the time. On the surface, it looks like they are trying to control their partner. But underneath? They are afraid of being abandoned. May be they were cheated on before. May be they grew up feeling insecure. Controlling the situation feels like protection. If they monitor everything, nothing bad can surprise them.

The behavior is control.
The core emotion is fear of loss.

➢ How uncertainty is part of life

Uncertainty has always been a part of human life, even in ancient times, shaping civilizations, decisions, and beliefs. In ancient agriculture, for example, farmers depended on the unpredictable patterns of rain and sunlight; a drought or flood could destroy crops, so they developed rituals and offerings to gods like **Ra** in Egypt or **Indra** in India to seek protection and favor, acknowledging that much was beyond their control. Similarly, in ancient navigation, sailors like the Phoenicians or Polynesians ventured into vast oceans without maps or compasses, relying on stars, winds, and currents; each voyage carried immense uncertainty, yet it also led to discoveries and trade networks. Even in politics and war, leaders such as **Alexander the Great** or the Roman generals faced uncertain outcomes in battles, where strategy, chance, and morale could turn the tide unexpectedly. Philosophers of the time, like **Socrates** and

Buddha, reflected on life's unpredictability, teaching that acceptance of uncertainty and focus on virtuous action or mindfulness was key to inner peace. These examples show that uncertainty has always been part of human existence, prompting creativity, courage, and philosophical reflection.

Life can change in an instant, which shows just how uncertain it truly is. In a single moment, you might receive a pop up message that you have selected in multinational company or government job you have been dreaming of, bringing joy and excitement.

After sometime, someone you love could be separated from you due to circumstances or even death, bringing sadness and loss. These sudden changes remind us that life is unpredictable, and nothing is guaranteed. these examples prove that life changes in a seconds.

When fear becomes identity

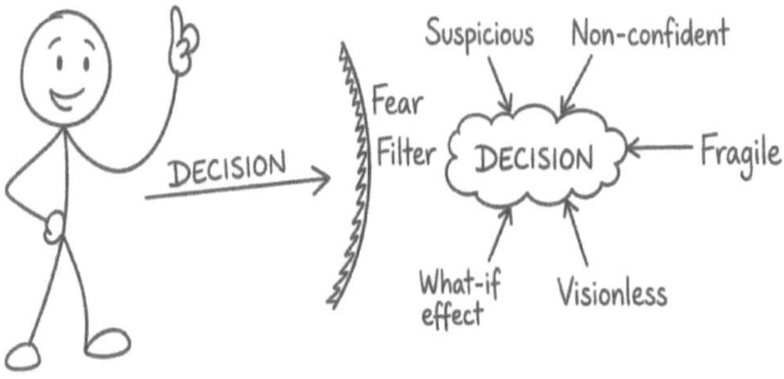

Fear becomes identity only when we let it. When we make every decision through its shadow, we start living small, shrinking from what could be. But courage begins the moment we refuse to be defined by fear. Step forward anyway. Speak, act, create, even with trembling hands. Every time we challenge the fear that tries to claim us, we reclaim ourselves. Fear does not define you—your choices, your resilience, your daring define you. Be the person who rises, not the person who hides.

If you continuously fear in future, it can develop into a phobia.

"When fear ceases to be just an emotion and begins to define who we are, it becomes our identity, shaping every choice, thought, and moment of life. True freedom lies in recognizing this and stepping beyond the 'if' that holds us captive."

An artist who receives harsh feedback early on may begin to identify as *"not creative enough."* They stop creating or sharing their work, letting fear shape their identity instead of their passion.

Now close your eyes and ask this question to yourself in your mind.

How have past experiences reinforced the belief that this fear is "who I am"?

➢ MENTAL LOOPS

Our minds have a way of looping—replaying the same "what ifs" and worries over and over, like a record stuck on fear. Anxiety whispers possibilities that may never happen, and overthinking convinces us we're preparing for the worst. But these loops are not who you are—they are a habit of the mind, not a reflection of your strength. The moment you notice the spiral and choose presence, action, or perspective, you break free.

Our minds love to loop. One idea comes, but fear, worry, and "what ifs", anxiety trap it, and to encounter previous idea another idea comes that too gets stuck in the same cycle. If we let it continue, we never reach the real power and potential of our thoughts. The way out is simple: think positively, speak encouraging words to yourself daily, and make it a habit. Each time you do, you break the loop, free your mind, and move closer to your goals.

"Life is yours, and it is entirely your responsibility to overcome and break this loop."

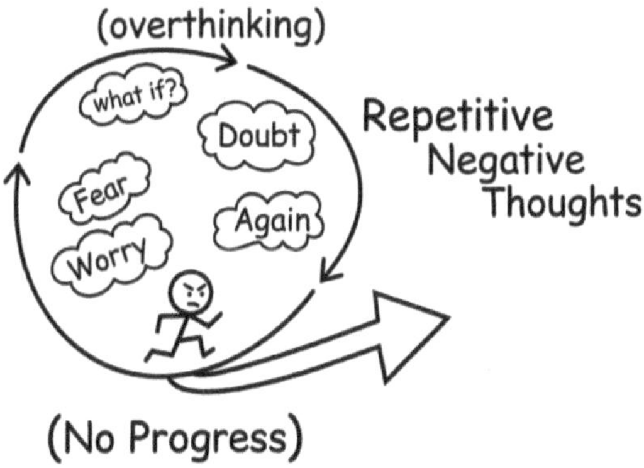

I will tell you with incident happens to us once in life.A professional makes a minor mistake during a presentation. Afterward, their thoughts repeatedly go:

"I embarrassed myself."

"Everyone thinks I'm incompetent."

"I can't do this job."

Even when there's no evidence for these beliefs, the mental loop keeps them stuck in anxiety and fear, letting the fear gradually become part of their identity.

➢ CATASTROPHIC THINKING

Catastrophic thinking means a pattern of thinking where your mind automatically jumps to the **worst possible outcome** of a situation, often imagining extreme or disastrous consequences, even when they are unlikely to happen.

Catastrophic thinking makes every small problem feel like a disaster waiting to happen. Your mind jumps to the worst-case scenario, imagining outcomes that may never come true, and traps you in fear and doubt. But your life is not controlled by imagined disasters—it is shaped by the actions you take today. Recognize these thoughts, challenge them, and take small steps forward. Each time you do, you shrink the mountain of fear and reclaim your power to think clearly, act confidently, and move toward your goals.

It is common in anxiety and overthinking, and it usually involves "what if" thoughts that make small problems feel huge.

Example:

In short, catastrophic thinking is **turning small worries into** You make a minor mistake at work and immediately think, "If I mess up, I'll get fired, ruin my career, and everyone will hate me."

The mind exaggerates the situation and focuses on worst-case scenarios instead of realistic outcomes.

Imagined disasters.

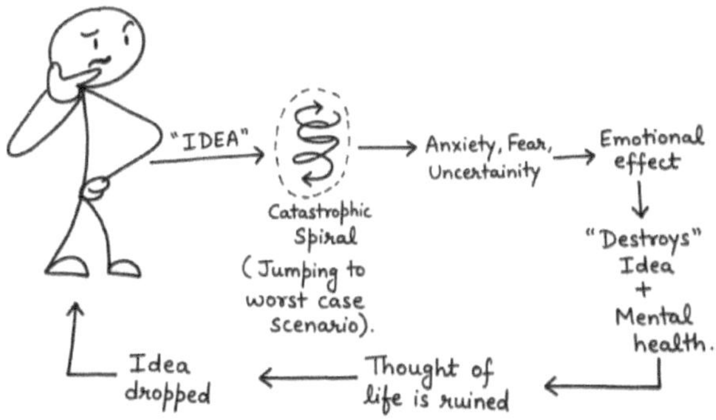

"This shows how you trapped in a catastrophic cycle, which can eventually harm your mental health if it continues unchecked. "to break this cycle you have to believe in yourself and believe that nothing is bigger than your will power.

➢ Anxiety,overthinking,paralysis

Anxiety – It starts as a natural response to a threat or uncertainty. When fear becomes a part of your identity, anxiety shifts from being occasional to constant, making your mind hyper-alert to "what could go wrong."

Overthinking – Anxiety fuels overthinking. You replay scenarios, analyze every choice, and imagine worst-case outcomes repeatedly. This creates a **mental loop** that reinforces the fear, making it feel like reality.

Paralysis (Decision or Action Paralysis) – Overthinking and constant anxiety can freeze you into inaction. You may feel stuck, unable to make choices, take risks, or move forward. This is often called **analysis paralysis**, and it strengthens the sense that fear is part of your identity: "I can't act because I am afraid."

Example in real life:
A person receives an invitation to speak at a conference. Anxiety arises: "What if I mess up?" Overthinking kicks in: "Will people judge me? What if I forget my points? What if they think I'm incompetent?" Eventually, the person cancels, feeling paralyzed. Over time, this reinforces the identity: *"I am not confident. I can't handle public speaking."*

anxiety sparks overthinking, overthinking fuels paralysis, and paralysis strengthens fear as identity.

If you want to come out from it just answer some of my questions. Just read it and then answer by your heart.

- What situations consistently trigger anxiety for me, and why?
- How does anxiety affect the choices I make daily?
- How often does overthinking prevent me from seeing solutions clearly?

- What patterns in my thinking indicate that fear is dominating my mind?
- In what areas of life do I feel stuck or frozen, and what fears are behind that paralysis?

➢ LABELS WE GIVE OURSELVES

Fear often enters quietly, but the labels we attach to it give it a voice that feels permanent. When you start saying "this is just who I am," you allow a temporary emotion to define a lifelong identity. Yet the truth is, fear is not a limitation—it is a signal that you are standing at the edge of growth. The moment you refuse to accept those limiting labels, you begin to reclaim yourself. You are not "incapable" or "weak"; you are someone learning, evolving, and pushing forward despite doubt. Let your actions speak louder than your fears, and remember—who you become is not decided by fear, but by the courage you choose in spite of it.

Think about my horse riding experience. Maybe in the beginning, the horse felt unpredictable to me, balance wasn't steady, and there was a moment of fear—maybe even a fall or a loss of control. In that moment, it's easy to label yourself: "I'm not good at this" or "I'm not meant for horse riding." That label doesn't come from truth—it comes from fear.

If i had held onto that label, i might have stopped riding altogether. But instead, every time i got back on the horse, i proved fear wrong .I learned how to balance, how to trust the horse, and most importantly, how to trust yourself. The fear didn't disappear instantly, but it stopped becoming my identity.

That's the power of breaking self-labels. You didn't become a rider because i had no fear— I became one because i refused to let fear define me.

student who once failed a math exam. After that experience, they start saying, "I'm bad at math." At first, it's just frustration—but over time, it becomes a label. Because of that belief, they avoid practicing, feel anxious in class, and stop trying altogether. Eventually, their performance reflects that fear, reinforcing the label they gave themselves.

But imagine if that same student chose a different perspective: instead of "I'm bad at math," they said, "I didn't understand this yet." That small shift changes everything. They begin to practice more, ask questions, and slowly improve. The fear is still there, but it no longer defines them.

This is how labels work in real life—they can either trap you in a fixed identity or open the door to growth.

What labels have I given myself out of fear rather than truth?

When did I start believing these labels about myself?

How have these labels limited my actions or choices?

Are these labels based on facts, or just past experiences and assumptions?

Who could I become if I stopped defining myself by fear?

Stay calm and answer these questions again with eyes closed,and think about your past life experiences.

"A label born from fear can only limit a life meant for growth."

PART-3

BREAKING THE "WHAT IF" CYCLE

I've had a lot of worries in my life, most of which never happened."

-----Mark Twain

A perfect reminder that most "what if" fears never become reality.

Reframing "what if"

Now that you understand the "what if" factor and the impact it can have on your thoughts and circumstances, it's time to take control of it. In this section, we will move beyond fear and learn how to transform negative "what if" thinking into positive, empowering possibilities. The same imagination that once created doubt can now create confidence. Are you ready to shift your mindset, challenge limiting thoughts, and turn uncertainty into opportunity? Let's begin the journey of converting negative "what ifs" into positive momentum.

➢ From "what if I fail?" to "what if I grow?", what if I learn?", to what if it work?"

Stop asking, "What if I fail?" That question keeps you trapped in fear. Ask instead, "What if I learn? What if it works? What if I grow stronger, wiser, braver?" Every challenge holds a lesson, every risk carries opportunity. Failure is not an ending—it is feedback. Fear is not a wall—it is a doorway. When you shift your questions, you shift your mindset. And when you shift your mindset, you open the door to a life you never thought possible or The moment you shift the question, you shift your power. And when you shift your power, you shift your life.

This we understand with a example:

When we were children in school, these thoughts often arose in our minds, especially during classroom activities. A similar feeling occurred during morning assembly or when students were asked to speak in front of others. Even when they had prepared well, fear of making a mistake or being judged by classmates sometimes

1. From "What if I fail?" → "What if I grow?"

Example:
A student wants to speak in front of the class but feels scared.

Old thought: *"What if I fail and everyone laughs?"*

New thought: *"What if I grow and become more confident at speaking?"*

Real outcome:
Even if the presentation is not perfect, the student becomes **better at public speaking each time**.

When I was writing this book, a thought often came to my mind: *What if no one reads it? What if the book turns out to be boring?*

However, the result turned out to be completely different. I wrote the book, and now you are reading it.

The same thing happens in business. People often think, *What if the business does not succeed? What if I face losses?* But if we let these doubts stop us, we may never begin.

Sometimes the fears we imagine never actually happen. The only way to know the result is to take the first step and move forward.

2. From "What if I fail?" → "What if I learn?"

Example:
Someone starts a small online business selling handmade products.

Old thought: *"What if nobody buys?"*

New thought: *"What if I learn how business, marketing, and customers work?"*

Real outcome:
Even if the first attempt doesn't make much money, the person **learns skills that help in the next attempt**.

3. From "What if I fail?" → "What if it works?"

Example:
A person wants to apply for a job at a big company.

Old thought: *"What if they reject me?"*

New thought: *"What if it works and I get the job?"*

Real outcome:
If they apply, there is **a real chance of success** that would never exist if they didn't try.

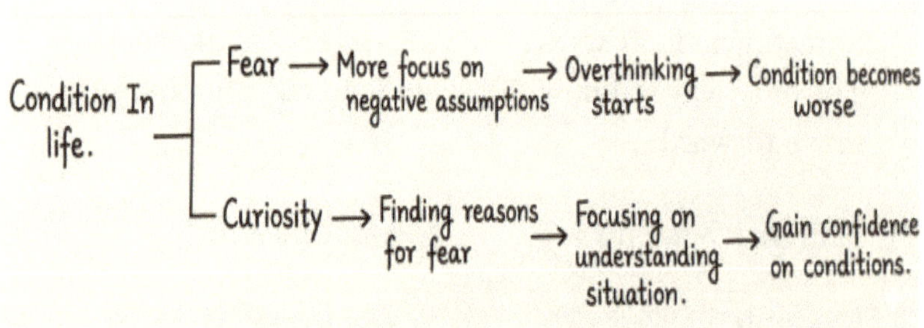

➢ COGNITIVE REFRAMING EXERCISES

Our brain works through systems and patterns. You may have heard about the subconscious mind, which plays an important role in shaping the systems that influence our daily lives. The subconscious mind stores repeated behaviors and gradually turns them into habits.

For example, earlier I had the habit of arriving late almost everywhere, including my classes when I was a student and even later when I started working as a teacher. Initially, it happened once or twice, but over time those repeated actions slowly turned into a habit. As this pattern developed, my brain began to justify the behavior by suggesting thoughts such as, "It is okay for today; next time I will be on time." However, that "next time" rarely came, and the habit continued.

In a similar way, many people develop the habit of checking their mobile phones every few minutes. Often they are not consciously aware of this behavior because it gradually becomes programmed into their minds. The brain starts treating it as a normal and automatic action, which leads them to check their phones repeatedly throughout the day.

On the other hand, habits can also be formed in a positive way. For example, if someone goes to the gym regularly at the same time every day, after about twenty days their mind and body begin to adjust to that routine. Gradually, their entire schedule aligns with that activity, and going to the gym at that particular time becomes a natural part of their daily life.

This shows that many of our behaviors operate at a subconscious level. Sometimes, without realizing it, we unintentionally adopt habits that may not be beneficial. Therefore, it is important to become aware of our daily behaviors and routines. To develop this awareness, we will now look at some exercises that can help us identify and understand our habits more clearly.

The ABCDE Model

A – Activating Event

This is the situation or event that happens.

Example:
You gave a presentation and someone criticized it.

B – Belief

This is the thought or belief you have about the event.

Example:
"I am not good at presentations."

C – Consequence

This is how you **feel and behave** because of that belief.

Example:

Feeling: Sad, embarrassed

Behavior: Avoid giving presentations in the future

D – Dispute

Here you **challenge the negative belief** by questioning it.

Ask questions like:

Is this belief completely true?

What evidence do I have?

Am I ignoring my strengths?

Example:
"I may have made some mistakes, but I have given good presentations before."

E – Effect (New Thinking)

After challenging the belief, you create a **more balanced thought**.

Example:
"I can improve my presentation skills with practice."

This leads to **better emotions and more confident behavior**.

1. The "Pause and Reframe" Exercise

This exercise helps people **stop automatic negative thinking**.

Steps:

When a negative thought appears, **pause for a moment**.

Ask yourself: *"Is there another way to look at this situation?"*

Replace the negative thought with a **more balanced thought**.

Example:

Automatic thought: "I made a mistake, I am not capable."

Reframed thought: "Mistakes are part of learning. I can improve next time."

This exercise trains the brain to **respond instead of reacting**.

2. The "Three Different Perspectives" Exercise

This activity helps people see a situation from **multiple viewpoints**.

Steps:
Write the situation and answer three questions:

My perspective: How do I see this situation?

Another person's perspective: How might someone else see it?

Neutral observer's perspective: What would an unbiased person say?

Example:
Situation: I received criticism.

My perspective: "They don't like my work."

Other perspective: "They want me to improve."

Neutral perspective: "Feedback can help develop better skills."

This exercise reduces **emotional bias**.

3. The "Silver Lining" Exercise

This exercise helps people **find positive meaning in difficult situations**.

Steps:

Write a challenging situation.

Ask yourself:

What can I learn from this?

How can this experience help me grow?

Example:
Situation: I failed in an exam.

Reframe:
"This experience shows me where I need to focus more, and it can help me prepare better next time."

This exercise builds **resilience and positive thinking**.

This exercise can be beneficial to some extent if you dedicate time to it and practice regularly.

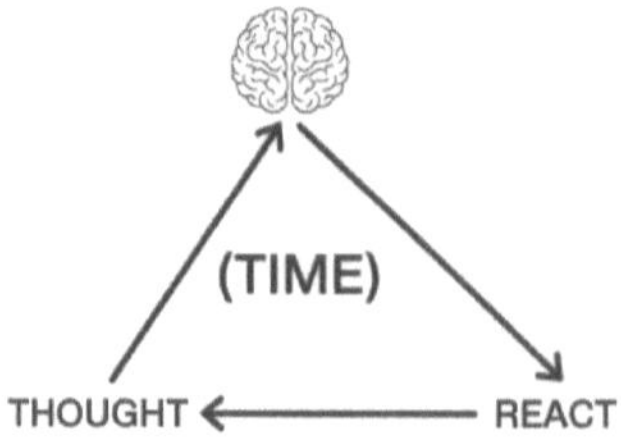

Believe me, you do have time. There is always a brief moment between a thought entering your mind and your reaction to it. If you develop the habit of recognizing that moment, you begin to shape and control yourself.

For example, when you suddenly feel angry, a thought first enters your mind and then you react. In that short space before you speak or act, you still have time. Even before uttering any word, you often pause—consciously or unconsciously—to decide what to say and what not to say. That moment shows that you have control over the situation. Therefore, train yourself to notice that small gap between thought and reaction. The more aware you become of it, the more control you gain over your words, emotions, and actions. Strive to be the person who recognizes that moment and uses it wisely.

Building emotional resilience

Building emotional resilience is about living a **life beyond "if"**—letting go of regrets, "what-ifs," and fears about things that didn't happen or could have happened differently. Instead of dwelling on missed opportunities or imagined outcomes, resilient people focus on what they **can control**, learn from setbacks, and take positive action. By accepting reality as it is, embracing challenges as opportunities to grow, and cultivating a mindset of adaptability and gratitude, we strengthen our ability to recover from adversity and move forward with confidence. Life beyond "if" is essentially a practice of emotional

➢ Self trust

Self-trust is the confidence in your own **judgment, abilities, and instincts** to make decisions, take action, and handle life's challenges. It means believing that you can rely on yourself, even when situations are uncertain or difficult.

Key aspects of self-trust include:

Listening to yourself: Paying attention to your feelings, intuition, and values.

Taking responsibility: Owning your choices and learning from mistakes without harsh self-judgment.

Consistency: Following through on promises you make to yourself, which builds inner reliability.

Confidence in decision-making: Trusting that you can handle consequences and adapt as needed.

Developing self-trust strengthens emotional resilience because it gives you an **inner anchor**—a sense that no matter what happens, you can navigate challenges with clarity and confidence.

One day, my friend asked me to teach him how to drive a car. I said yes, even though I didn't know how to drive . He insisted, and I couldn't bring myself to say no. He took me to his grandmother's house, which was located on a very narrow lane—so narrow that even a professional driver would struggle to navigate it. His whole family was waiting, expecting me to start the car and drive. At that moment, I told myself, *"Vaibhav, you can do this. This is not a plane you need to fly; it's just a car."* Jokingly, I even thought, *"I can fly a plane too!"* I took a deep breath, got into the car, and started driving. Despite not knowing how to drive, I managed to take the car out of the narrow lane successfully. His grandmother even commented that vaibhav is such a professional driver!

But the challenge wasn't over. On the way back, the lane was crowded with milk sellers who told me come from this side, that way which required cutting through a tricky area. I navigated carefully and finally parked the car at his home, which had an L-shaped parking spot where even a small mistake could damage the car. That four-hour ride was a complete success, and it taught me the power of **self-trust**. I realized that talking to yourself, motivating yourself, and trusting your own abilities can help you overcome challenges you never thought you could handle. Remarkably, this single experience carried me through the next three months and was how I truly learned to drive. Even though my friend believes that he learned to drive only because of me, that isn't entirely true. I guided him but as iam guiding to myself.

➢ Self compassion

Remember, being kind to yourself is not weakness—it's strength. Every stumble, every mistake, every moment of doubt is part of your journey, not a measure of your worth. Treat yourself with the same patience and understanding you would offer a friend, and you'll discover a quiet power within you. When you embrace your imperfections with compassion, you free yourself to learn, grow, and move forward without fear. Today, give yourself permission to be human, to heal, and to keep going—because your potential is greater than any setback.

"It is often said that if you do not respect yourself, no other person will respect you."

Self compassion=self love=boost confidence=closer to goals.

➢ ACCEPTING IMPERFECTION

Accepting imperfection means understanding that no one is flawless and that mistakes are a natural part of being human. Instead of constantly criticizing yourself for what you lack, you learn to appreciate your efforts and progress. When you accept your imperfections, you free yourself from unrealistic expectations and unnecessary pressure. This mindset allows you to grow, learn from your experiences, and become stronger with every challenge. True confidence comes not from being perfect, but from embracing who you are while continuously striving to improve.

Sometimes a student studies very hard for an exam but still does not get the expected marks. Instead of thinking, *"I am not good enough,"* accepting imperfection means understanding that mistakes and setbacks are part of learning. The student reflects on what went wrong, learns from the experience, and prepares better for the next exam. By accepting that no one is perfect, the student grows stronger, more confident.

Life can also be compared to an exam. Striving for perfection can be a positive quality, but only to a certain extent. It should never come at the cost of your mental peace or health. When the desire to be perfect becomes excessive, it can turn into a burden. In reality, it is not always possible for every task to be completed perfectly or without mistakes. Therefore, it is important to understand your limits and recognize where to draw the line between healthy ambition and harmful perfectionism.

Courage in small steps

"Great palaces are built brick by brick."

"Until we build our reputation and achieve the goals we aspire to, we must move forward with courage in every step, guided by confidence. When we have nothing else, these qualities become the most powerful tools we possess."

Courage is not always about taking giant leaps; it often begins with small, quiet steps. Every time you choose to try again after failing, speak up when it feels uncomfortable, or step slightly beyond your comfort zone, you are showing courage. These small actions may seem insignificant at first, but over time they build confidence, strength, and resilience. Remember, great achievements are rarely the result of one bold move—they are the result of many small, brave steps taken consistently. Keep moving forward, no matter how small the step, because each one brings you closer to the person you aspire to become.

A person who is afraid of public speaking may not suddenly give a speech in front of a large audience. Instead, they begin with small steps—first sharing their ideas with a close friend, then speaking in a small group, and later presenting in front of a class or team. Each small step helps them build confidence and gradually reduce their fear. Over time, these small acts of courage allow them to overcome their anxiety and speak confidently in public.

This shows that **courage often grows through small, consistent actions rather than one big moment of bravery.**

- Micro bravery

Micro-bravery refers to small, everyday acts of courage that may seem minor but gradually build confidence and resilience. Instead of waiting for one big, heroic moment, micro-bravery is about taking small steps outside your comfort zone—such as asking a question in a meeting, expressing your opinion respectfully, admitting a mistake, or trying something new even when you feel uncertain.

These small acts of courage might not look dramatic, but they play a powerful role in personal growth. Each time you practice micro-bravery, you strengthen your confidence and reduce the fear of failure or judgment. Over time, these small courageous actions accumulate and prepare you to handle bigger challenges with greater strength and self-belief.

A new employee at a company feels nervous about sharing their ideas in team meetings. Instead of staying silent, they start by suggesting a small improvement to a project via email. Later, they share a thought during a short team discussion, and gradually they speak up more confidently in larger meetings. Each small act of courage strengthens their confidence and helps them become an active, respected contributor.

➢ EXPOSURE TO FEAR

This pattern often begins in childhood. For example, when a teacher announces a test the next day, some children may skip class out of fear. Over time, similar situations occur repeatedly, and we may develop a habit of avoiding challenges instead of facing them. This tendency to run from fear can continue into adulthood, shaping how we respond to difficult or stressful situations throughout life.

Once we understand that exposure to fear helps our minds and bodies adapt, the next step is to act with courage—one small step at a time. Every tiny action, whether it's speaking up, trying something new, or facing a mild fear, is a victory that strengthens our confidence. These small wins accumulate, showing us that we are capable of more than we imagine. With each step, fear loses its power, and courage grows, motivating us to face even greater challenges with determination and hope.

When you avoid something you fear, your brain never gets a chance to learn that it might actually be safe

Types of exposure

Gradual (systematic): step-by-step (e.g., fear of dogs → look at pictures → watch from afar → stand near → interact)

Flooding: jumping straight into the fear (less commonly used because it's intense)

Imaginal exposure: visualizing the fear (used when real exposure isn't possible)

Interoceptive exposure: triggering physical sensations (often for panic)

Why it works

It's based on a principle called Habituation:

Repeated exposure reduces emotional response

The fear signal weakens over time

Example

If someone fears public speaking:

Practice alone

Speak in front of a mirror

Talk to a friend

Present to a small group

Speak to a larger audience

Each step builds confidence and reduces fear.

Important note

Exposure works best when:

It's **gradual and repeated**

You **stay in the situation long enough** for anxiety to decrease

You **don't escape too quickly**, or the fear stays reinforced

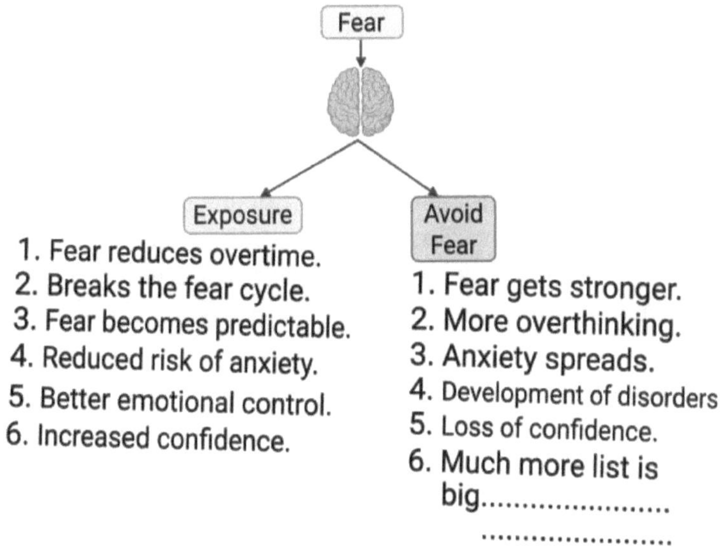

➢ ACTION BEFORE CONFIDENCE

Don't wait until you feel confident to start—just take the first step. Confidence grows when you act, not when you hesitate. Even small efforts can lead to big changes over time. Trust yourself, keep moving forward, and remember that every action you take makes you stronger and more capable.

Well begun is half done." — Aristotle

Action builds confidence, and confidence helps you achieve your dreams. Instead of waiting to feel ready, focus on taking small steps. Over time, your confidence will grow naturally.

I experienced this in my own life. I started teaching history at a very young age—just 18. In the beginning, many students doubted me and even made fun of me, questioning what I could teach at such a young age. However, I did not let their words affect me. I continued working and teaching at different places, and gradually, my confidence grew. Today, some of those same students, who are still in touch, treat me with respect.

When you begin any journey, understand that if you start with even 10% confidence, the world may try to shake it. The key is to protect and hold onto that small amount of confidence. If you can do that, you are ready for the next stage of life. That 10% will grow to 40%, then 60%, 80%, and even 99%. And that 1% to gain that 1% confidence, it again takes soo much effort sometimes it takes whole of life and strength because doing something with 100%

surety it took lots of effort. Reaching 100% confidence, effort, and sometimes a lifetime of learning and persistence

. Stay consistent, keep taking action, and believe in your growth.

#Letting go of outcome attachment

Stop worrying about "what if" and the results you can't control. True growth comes when you focus on your actions and give your best, without being tied to the outcome. Every effort you make teaches you something, builds your strength, and brings you closer to your goals. Let go of expectations, trust the process, and keep moving forward—life opens up when you act with courage, not fear.

Imagine you want to start a small business. If you focus only on "What if I fail?" or "What if no one likes my product?" you might never start. Instead, you take action: you plan, create your product, and reach out to customers. You don't obsess over every possible result; you focus on learning, improving, and giving your best.

- Over time, your efforts pay off. Some things succeed, some don't, but each step makes you stronger, wiser, and more confident. By letting go of outcome attachments that success comes from disciplined effort, selfless action, and commitment, rather than from the expectation of rewards.
- Don't let "what if" stop you from moving forward. Success doesn't come from worrying about results—it comes from taking action and giving your best every day. When you focus on effort, the results

will follow, and you'll discover your true potential.

- Focus on effort, not results

"You have a right to work, but never to the fruit of work. You should never engage in action for the sake of reward, nor should you long for inaction." — Bhagavad Gita (Chapter 2, Verse 47)

In India, the famous sacred text **Bhagavad Gita** teaches the

timeless principle of focusing on one's actions rather than the results. In this divine scripture, the Hindu god **Lord Krishna** advises Arjuna to perform his duties with sincerity and dedication, without attachment to the outcomes. This guidance eACTION BEFORE CONFIDENCE

Don't wait until you feel confident to start—just take the first step. Confidence grows when you act, not when you hesitate. Even small efforts can lead to big changes over time. Trust yourself, keep moving forward, and remember that every action you take makes you stronger and more capable.

Well begun is half done." — Aristotle

Action builds confidence, and confidence helps you achieve your dreams. Instead of waiting to feel ready, focus on taking small steps. Over time, your confidence will grow naturally.

I experienced this in my own life. I started teaching history at a very young age—just 18. In the beginning, many students doubted me and even made fun of me, questioning what I could teach at such a young age. However, I did not let their words affect me. I continued working and teaching at different places, and gradually, my confidence grew. Today, some of those same students, who are still in touch, treat me with respect.

When you begin any journey, understand that if you start with even 10% confidence, the world may try to shake it. The key is to protect and hold onto that small amount of confidence. If you can do that, you are ready for the next stage of life. That 10% will grow to 40%, then 60%, 80%, and even 99%. And that 1% to gain that 1% confidence, it again takes soo much effort sometimes it takes whole of life and strength because doing something with 100% surety it took lots of effort. Reaching 100% confidence, effort, and sometimes a lifetime of learning and persistence. Stay consistent, keep taking action, and believe in your growth.

Don't wait to feel ready—act first. Confidence isn't a magic switch; it's forged in motion. Every step you take, even when unsure, builds strength, skill, and belief. Fear fades when you move, doubt shrinks when you try, and success comes to those who act before they feel prepared. Start now—confidence will catch up with every bold move.

➢ PROCESSS OVER PERFECTION

Success doesn't come from trying to be perfect—it comes from focusing on the **process**. When you concentrate on consistent effort, learning, and improvement, progress naturally follows. Perfection can create fear, stress, and hesitation, but embracing the process allows you to grow, experiment, and adapt. Every step, even small or imperfect, moves you closer to your goals. Value action, persistence, and learning, and let perfection take care of itself.

- **Learning a musical instrument** – No one becomes a great pianist or guitarist overnight. Regular practice, even with mistakes, improves skill over time. Focusing on the process of learning, rather than perfect performance, leads to mastery.

- **Fitness and exercise** – You won't get a perfect body instantly. Consistent workouts, proper nutrition, and gradual improvement matter more than flawless results. Progress comes from sticking to the process.

Perfection often leaves you never fully satisfied, because there is always something more to improve. Focusing on the **process**, however, allows you to understand where you stand at every step and continuously sharpen your skills. While striving for perfection can be valuable, it cannot be applied to everything. Embracing the process ensures steady growth, learning from each step, and a sense of progress, rather than constant frustration over unattainable perfection.

➢ DETACHING FROM EXTERNAL VALIDATION

Stop measuring your worth by what others think of you. True confidence comes from within, not from applause or approval. Focus on your growth, effort, and values, and let your actions speak for themselves. When you stop seeking validation, you gain freedom, clarity, and strength to pursue your goals without fear. Trust yourself, keep moving forward, and let your inner conviction guide your journey.

Many people start working out to impress others or get praise for their appearance. But when you focus on **your own health, energy, and well-being**, you stay consistent even if nobody notices. Over time, the results—strength, stamina, and confidence—come naturally, and your motivation is driven by self-care, not approval from others This shows that when your focus is on **your own effort and growth**, rather than others' opinions, you achieve lasting results and inner satisfaction.

"Trust yourself deeply. When all is said and done, the only person lying on that deathbed with you is you. Make sure you are in good company."

Prioritize your health and your mind. Once they are gone, you become a prisoner within your own body. True freedom starts with how you treat yourself today."

➢ Society and its questions

There comes a moment in everyone's life when the questions don't feel like curiosity anymore—they feel like judgment.

"Why are you still single?"
"When will you settle down?"
"Why aren't you earning more?"
"What are you even doing with your life?"

At first, they seem harmless. But over time, they start planting seeds of doubt. You begin to question yourself—not because you were unsure, but because the world made you feel like you should be.

But here's the truth:

Not every question deserves a place in your mind.

Why Society Asks These Questions

Most people don't ask questions to understand you—they ask to compare you.

They measure your life based on:

- Their beliefs
- Their timelines
- Their fears

And when your life doesn't match their expectations, they question it.

But remember this:

"Their questions reflect their mindset—not your potential."

The Hidden Pressure Behind Simple Questions

A simple question can carry heavy expectations:

- "Why aren't you married?" → *You're late in life*
- "Why not a better job?" → *You're not successful enough*
- "Why are you different?" → *You should fit in*

Over time, these questions create pressure to:

- Rush decisions
- Doubt your path
- Compare your journey

How to Respond Without Losing Yourself

1. Stay Grounded

You don't need to react to everything. A calm mind is your greatest strength.

2. Answer with Confidence

You don't need perfect answers—just honest ones:

- "I'm working on my goals step by step."
- "I'm focusing on what truly matters to me."
- "I believe my timing is right for me."

3. Set Boundaries

Not every question deserves an answer.
You can simply say:

- "I'd rather not get into that."
- "I'm figuring things out in my own way."

That's not rude—that's self-respect.

- "I'd rather not get into that."
- "I'm figuring things out in my own way."

That's not rude—that's self-respect.

- "I'd rather not get into that."
- "I'm figuring things out in my own way."

That's not rude—that's self-respect.

PART-4

Living Beyond Fear

"Expose yourself to your deepest fear; after that, fear has no power."

Jim Morrison

#The Freedom Of Acceptance

Freedom of acceptance in the concept of living beyond fear refers to the ability to embrace reality as it is, without resisting or denying uncomfortable experiences such as uncertainty, pain, or failure. Instead of trying to control everything or avoid fear, a person learns to accept their thoughts and emotions, recognizing that fear is a natural part of life. This acceptance reduces the power fear holds, allowing individuals to act with clarity and courage rather than hesitation. Influenced by ideas found in Acceptance and Commitment Therapy and Mindfulness, this approach teaches that true freedom comes not from eliminating fear, but from no longer being controlled by it. As a result, a person can live more authentically, make meaningful choices, and move forward in life with resilience and inner peace.

In a relationship can be seen when someone goes through a breakup. Initially, they may feel intense fear—fear of being alone, fear of not finding love again, or fear of losing emotional security. They might resist the situation by holding on, overthinking, or refusing to let go. However, when they begin to practice acceptance, they acknowledge the reality: "This relationship has ended, and it's painful, but I can still move forward." Instead of trying to control the past or avoid the pain, they allow themselves to feel the emotions and gradually focus on healing, self-growth, and new possibilities.

➢ Life is unpredictable

There is a quiet freedom in accepting that life is unpredictable. The moment you stop resisting uncertainty, you release the burden of needing everything to be controlled or perfect. Acceptance does not mean giving up—it means understanding that not everything is in your hands, and that is okay. When you embrace this truth, fear begins to lose its grip, and you create space for peace, resilience, and growth. You start to flow with life instead of fighting it, trusting that whatever comes, you have the strength to face it. In that acceptance, you find a deeper sense of freedom—the freedom to live fully, without being held back by the fear of the unknown.

Life is unpredictable—full of unexpected turns, challenges, and moments that test your strength. You cannot always control what happens, but you can control how you respond. When uncertainty brings fear, do not let it define who you are. Instead, let it shape your courage. Every obstacle carries a lesson, and every setback holds the potential for growth. Trust yourself enough to keep moving forward, even when the path is unclear. Because in the end, it is not the unpredictability of life that determines your story, but the resilience and belief you choose to carry through it.

If life is unpredictable, worrying only steals energy from the present without changing the outcome. Worry assumes you can control what cannot be controlled, but life's uncertainties are beyond anyone's full grasp. Instead of spending time imagining what might go wrong, focus on what you *can* influence—your actions, your mindset, and your choices. Worry adds weight; acceptance brings freedom. By letting go of unnecessary fear, you free yourself to respond with clarity, courage, and creativity, turning life's unpredictability from a source of stress into an opportunity for growth and discovery.

You wake up on time, plan your route carefully, but traffic or delays cause you to miss it. In that moment, panic and worry often arise: *"Now I'll be late, everything will go wrong."* But the reality is, worrying doesn't get the bus to come faster. You adjust: maybe you take the next bus, call ahead, or change your plan. By letting go of the worry, you conserve your energy to act calmly and solve the situation.

This happens in countless ways in life—missed appointments, unexpected work challenges, sudden rain, or last-minute changes. Life is unpredictable, but worrying doesn't prevent the unexpected—it only makes navigating it harder. Accepting unpredictability and focusing on what you *can* control is what turns obstacles into manageable moments.

"You cannot control everything in life, but you can control how you respond."

➢ Acceptance is not weakness

acceptance is not weakness; it is strength in its purest form. Accepting life as it comes does not mean giving up, resigning, or being passive. It means recognizing reality clearly, letting go of what you cannot control, and choosing to respond wisely. True strength lies in facing life's uncertainties without resistance, embracing challenges without fear, and moving forward with clarity and courage. Acceptance frees your mind and energy to focus on growth, solutions, and meaningful action, turning unpredictability from a source of stress into a pathway for resilience and empowerment.

Because many people confuse acceptance with giving up or being weak. In reality, acceptance is an active choice—it requires awareness, courage, and self-control. When you accept something, you are not saying "I like this" or "I approve"; you are saying, "I recognize reality as it is, and I will respond wisely."

Without acceptance, energy is wasted on resistance, denial, or frustration. With acceptance, you gain clarity, reduce unnecessary stress, and free yourself to take meaningful action. That's why acceptance is **strength**, not weakness—it takes more courage to face reality and act wisely than to ignore it or fight what you cannot change.

To accept life's truths is not submission—it is the nobility of the mind, the hallmark of a ruler in his own life."

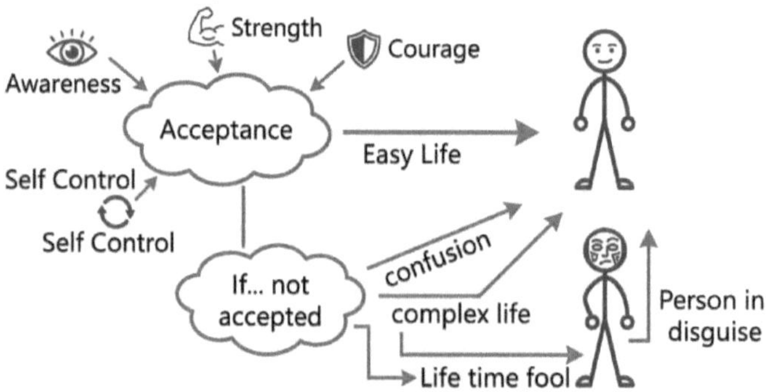
Strength
Courage
Awareness
Acceptance
Easy Life
Self Control
Self Control
If... not accepted
confusion
complex life
Person in disguise
Life time fool

➢ Surrender vs giving up

Surrender is a conscious act of strength. It means acknowledging reality as it is, letting go of what you cannot control, and choosing to respond with clarity and wisdom. Surrender is about aligning with life, not resisting it. It opens the door to growth, learning, and inner peace.

Giving up, on the other hand, comes from fear, frustration, or hopelessness. It is a passive act where you stop trying, stop learning, or stop believing in your potential. Giving up shrinks possibilities and strengthens limitations.

The key difference: Surrender is **active and empowering**, while giving up is **passive and limiting**. One frees you to move forward; the other holds you back.

Surrender is strength; giving up is defeat. One frees you to grow, the other chains you to fear."

Health & Fitness:

Giving up: You fail to meet a fitness goal once or twice and decide you'll never get in shape.

Surrender: You accept your current state, adjust your routine realistically, and commit to gradual improvement, embracing the process instead of quitting.

Designing a bold or fearless life

A bold and fearless life is not the absence of fear—it is the courage to act despite it. It begins with a clear vision of what you want and the willingness to face the fears that try to hold you back. Fear loses its power the moment you recognize it as a feeling, not your identity. By challenging limiting beliefs, taking courageous steps, embracing failure as a lesson, and cultivating resilience, you shape a life defined by growth, strength, and purpose. Surround yourself with positivity, move forward with patience, and remember: every act of bravery, no matter how small, builds the fearless life you were meant to live.

*How to Design bold and fearless life

1. Clarify Your Vision

Know what you truly want—your values, goals, and passions. A clear vision acts as a compass when fear tries to distract you.

2. Identify Your Fears

Acknowledge what scares you. Label them ("fear of failure," "fear of judgment") so they remain feelings you can manage, not identities that define you.

3. Challenge Limiting Beliefs

Replace self-limiting thoughts like "I can't do this" with empowering ones like "I'm learning" or "I can grow." Question any label you've given yourself out of fear.

4. Take Courageous Action

Boldness is built through action, not intention. Start small—speak up, try something new, or take calculated risks. Every step forward strengthens confidence.

5. Embrace Failure as Feedback

See mistakes as lessons, not proof of incapability. Failure is a natural part of growth and a sign that you are pushing your boundaries.

6. Practice Resilience and Patience

Life is unpredictable. Accept setbacks, learn from them, and keep moving forward. Resilience turns challenges into opportunities.

7. Surround Yourself with Strength

Spend time with people who inspire courage and growth. Avoid environments that reinforce fear or self-doubt. Strength is not in avoiding challenges, but in facing them with an open heart and steady mind."

➢ Choosing values over comfort

Choosing values over comfort is the quiet courage that shapes a meaningful life. It means standing firm in what you believe, even when the easier path tempts you to give in. Growth rarely happens in comfort—it happens when you push through doubt, face challenges, and stay true to your principles. Every time you choose honesty over convenience, discipline over distraction, or purpose over fear, you build strength and self-respect. In the end, comfort fades, but the life you create through your values becomes your true reward.

Choosing values over comfort is a powerful act of self-respect. It means refusing to let fear, laziness, or temporary ease decide your path. When you choose discipline over distraction, truth over silence, and purpose over popularity, you step into a stronger version of yourself. It won't always feel good—there will be moments of doubt, struggle, and sacrifice—but those are the moments that define your character. Every uncomfortable choice you make in favor of your values is an investment in a life you can be proud of. Over time, what once felt hard becomes your strength, and what once seemed like sacrifice becomes your greatest achievement.

A simple example of choosing values over comfort is a student who decides to study for an important exam instead of scrolling on their phone or watching movies. It's much more comfortable to relax and avoid the pressure, but the student chooses discipline and responsibility because they value their future and goals.

Another example is speaking up when you see someone being treated unfairly. Staying quiet might feel safer and more comfortable, but choosing to stand for what's right shows courage and integrity.

In both cases, the easy option gives short-term comfort, but the harder choice builds character and leads to long-term respect and success.

➢ Creating a purpose driven life

Creating a purpose-driven life means choosing to live with intention, not just going through the motions. It starts with understanding what truly matters to you—your values, your passions, and the kind of person you want to become. Instead of chasing temporary comfort or approval, you begin to make choices that align with a deeper meaning. This might mean setting clear goals, embracing discipline, and staying committed even when things get difficult.

A purpose-driven life isn't about having everything figured out; it's about moving forward with clarity and direction. You learn to see challenges as opportunities to grow and setbacks as lessons rather than failures. When your actions match your values, even small steps feel meaningful, and your life gains a sense of fulfillment that comfort alone can never provide. Over time, you don't just live—you build a life that reflects who you truly are and what you stand for.

One Goal Per Month principle

The **One Goal Per Month principle** is a simple yet powerful way to stay focused and make consistent progress in life. In this approach, you choose one clear goal for each month and dedicate your time, energy, and attention fully to achieving it. Instead of trying to do everything at once, you concentrate on a single priority, which increases your chances of success.

Throughout the month, you not only work towards your goal but also keep track of the efforts, habits, and sacrifices you make along the way. This helps you stay accountable and understand the value of your hard work. The key rule of this system is to complete the chosen goal within the month before moving on to the next one.

At the end of the month, you reflect on your progress, learn from your experience, and then set a new goal for the following month. By repeating this cycle, you build discipline, clarity, and a strong sense of purpose—one goal at a time.

Month: January
Goal: Improve physical fitness

You decide that for this entire month, your only main focus is getting fit. You create a simple plan—exercise for 30 minutes daily, avoid junk food, and maintain a consistent sleep schedule.

Throughout the month, you stay committed:

You wake up early even when you feel lazy

You skip unhealthy snacks and choose better food

You reduce time on your phone to make space for workouts

You also write down your efforts and sacrifices, like missing late-night movies, pushing through tiredness, and staying disciplined on difficult days.

By the end of the month, you complete your goal—you feel healthier, stronger, and more confident.

➢ Daily habits to reduce fear

Day 1: Awareness & Journaling

Morning: Write down any "what if" thoughts that come to mind.

Task: For each thought, note one small action you *can* take today to address it.

Evening: Reflect on whether the fear came true or not. Most likely, it didn't.

Day 2: Mindful Breathing

Morning (5 min): Sit quietly, focus on your breath. Inhale 4 sec, hold 2 sec, exhale 6 sec.

Whenever fear arises: Take 3 deep mindful breaths before reacting.

Evening: Note one moment when you used this breathing technique and how it helped.

Day 3: Action Over Worry

Morning: Choose one fear or "what if" scenario today.

Task: Take **one small action** toward it, no matter how tiny.

Evening: Write down how it felt and what you learned. Even a small step counts.

Day 4: Physical Reset

Morning or Afternoon: Do 20–30 minutes of movement (walk, run, yoga, strength training).

Task: Pair movement with positive self-talk: "I am stronger than my fears."

Evening: Reflect on your energy and mood—movement reduces fear-related tension.

Day 5: Limit Negative Input

Morning: Identify one source of fear-inducing input (news, social media, conversations).

Task: Limit or avoid it today. Replace it with uplifting, solution-focused content.

Evening: Write how avoiding negativity affected your thoughts and emotions.

Day 6: Reflection & Gratitude

Morning: Write down three things you are grateful for or proud of.

Task: When a "what if" thought comes, acknowledge it, then shift focus to gratitude.

Evening: Review your journal: note situations where fear didn't control your actions.

Day 7: Consolidation & Planning

Morning: Identify patterns—what triggers "what if" thoughts, what actions help?

Task: Make a small **action plan for the next week** using what worked this week.

Evening: Celebrate any small victories. Reflect: "I am learning to face fear, step by step."

When 'what if' becomes 'why not'????

"What if" becomes **"why not"** the moment you stop seeing fear as a warning and start seeing it as a challenge.

It happens when:

You realize most of your fears never actually come true

You build confidence by taking small actions again and again

You shift your focus from *possible failure* to *possible growth*

You trust yourself enough to handle whatever happens

At first, your mind says, *"What if I fail?"*
But with practice, it changes to, *"Why not try?"*

Because you understand:

Even if you fail, you will learn

Even if it's hard, you will grow

Even if it's uncertain, you will figure it out

In simple words:
"What if" is driven by fear.
"Why not" is driven by courage and belief.

A person has always wanted to start working out and get fit, but every day their mind says, *"What if I can't stay consistent? What if I quit like before? What if it's too hard?"* So they keep delaying and staying in their comfort zone.

One day, they change the question: *"Why not start with just 10 minutes today? Why not give myself one real chance?"*

They begin—just a short workout. It feels tough, but they finish it. The next day, they show up again. Slowly, days turn into weeks, and weeks into a habit.

After a month, they look back and realize—they didn't need perfect confidence to start. They just needed to begin.

Lesson: "What if" keeps you stuck in imagination.
"Why not" gets you moving in reality

➢ Risk taking mindset

A **risk-taking mindset** is the ability to move forward despite uncertainty, fear, or the possibility of failure. It doesn't mean being careless—it means being brave enough to take **calculated risks** that can lead to growth, success, and new opportunities.

People with this mindset don't ask, *"What if everything goes wrong?"*
They ask, *"What can I gain if this works—and what will I learn if it doesn't?"*

They understand that:

Staying in the comfort zone feels safe but limits growth

Every opportunity involves some level of risk

Failure is not the end—it's feedback and experience

For example, applying for a job you feel underqualified for, starting something new, or speaking up with your ideas—all require risk. But these are the moments that create progress.

A risk-taking mindset is built by:

Taking small, consistent risks daily

Accepting that uncertainty is part of life

Focusing on learning instead of perfection

Trusting yourself to handle outcomes

<u>In simple words</u>:

No risk = no growth.

Small risks today = big confidence tomorrow

1. The Startup Leap

"I once walked away from a stable job to launch a startup. Friends thought I was crazy—but I had a vision I couldn't ignore. The first year was filled with uncertainty, sleepless nights, and tough decisions. Today, looking back, that risk was the turning point that defined my career.

➢ Becoming the author of your life

You are not just living life—you are writing it, one decision at a time. Every choice you make becomes a sentence, every habit a paragraph, and every challenge a turning point in your story. There will be moments of doubt, setbacks, and confusion, but those are not the end—they are the plot twists that make your journey meaningful. Don't wait for the perfect moment or someone else's approval. Take the pen in your own hands, trust your voice, and start shaping the life you truly want. Your story doesn't have to be perfect—it just has to be yours.

Some important things to remember.

- Life is yours.
- You are the author of your life.
- As long as you have breath, you can do anything.
- Believe in yourself, and only yourself.
- Take care of your health.
- If you are unhealthy, it will affect your mentality.
- Do not do work or take a job that destroys your mental peace.
- Choose growth over comfort.
- Stay strong in difficult times.
- Keep moving forward, no matter wha

 # Final chapter: Even if

"I am the master of my fate, I am the captain of my soul."

— William Ernest Henley

➢ Even if I fail, I will survive

Even if I fail, I will survive. There will be days when everything feels heavy, when my efforts seem wasted and my strength feels gone—but I will still hold on. I will remind myself that failure does not define me; it refines me. Every tear, every setback, every moment of doubt is shaping a stronger version of me. I may bend under pressure, but I will not break. Deep inside, I know I have the power to rise again, to rebuild, and to keep moving forward. Because no matter how many times life knocks me down, I will always find a way to stand back up and continue my story.

Michael Jordan. Early in his career, he was cut from his high school varsity team—essentially a major setback for a young athlete. But instead of giving up, he practiced harder, kept improving, and eventually became one of the greatest basketball players of all time.

His story shows that even if you “fail” at first, survival—and growth—comes from persistence, learning from mistakes, and refusing to quit

➢ Even if I'am rejected, I'am still worthy

***Rejection doesn't define your value*.**

No rejection can erase your value. Every setback is a setup for a comeback. You are stronger than your failures, braver than your fears, and more capable than you realize. Stand tall, keep moving, and never let anyone else define your worth—because you are enough, right now, exactly as you are.

Every "no" is a lesson.
Your worth is never defined by others—rise, try again, and shine

- "Rejection is a detour, not a dead end."
- "One 'no' doesn't erase your potential."
- "Fall, learn, rise stronger."
- "Keep moving—your breakthrough is ahead."
- "Your value is yours; no one can take it away."
- What did I learn from this experience?
- What can I do differently next time?
- Does this change my value or worth?
- What strengths did I use or discover in this situation?
- How can this "no" guide me toward a better opportunity?

- Am I holding onto something I can let go of?
- What small step can I take right now to keep moving forward.

"If you can answer these questions in your mind, they will bring clarity.

Congrats! you are now in a good mood.

If not think again on these questions.

➢ Even if i lose, I can rebuild

Even if I lose, I have the strength to rebuild and come back stronger."

Even if I lose, I will not be defeated. Every setback is a lesson, every failure a stepping stone. I have the strength, courage, and resilience to rebuild what's broken and rise even stronger. Losing is not the end—it is an opportunity to learn, grow, and come back better than before. I trust myself, I trust the process, and I know that with persistence, determination, and belief, I can overcome anything and achieve what I am meant to.

"I may lose, but I will rise. I rebuild, I grow, I become stronger."

You can repeat this every morning or whenever you feel discouraged to boost confidence and resilience.

Following steps will help you:

Step 1: Accept & Learn

Acknowledge the loss and ask yourself: *What can I learn from this?*

Step 2: Take a Small Action

Do one simple thing today that moves you forward, even if it's tiny.

Step 3: Keep the Mindset Positive

Remind yourself: *"I may have lost, but I can rebuild and grow stronger."*

Whenever you stuck in these situations just take deep breath and sit alone and ask questions to yourself but don't go in deep with yourself because more and more you answer questions you will be relaxed if not then take a 1hr sleep I know it will not come but you first work is to make silent ,relax your mind.

Best of luck I know you are strong and handle the situation wisely yess you……..

➢ Even if life changes, I can adapt

"Even if life changes, I can adapt and thrive."

It's about resilience—accepting change, staying flexible, and finding ways to grow no matter what life throws at you. Change isn't a threat; it's an opportunity to become stronger and wiser.

Even if life changes, I will not break. Change is a natural part of life, and I have the strength and flexibility to adapt. Every new challenge is an opportunity to learn, grow, and discover new possibilities. I trust myself to navigate uncertainty, find solutions, and keep moving forward. No matter what life brings, I can adjust, thrive, and become stronger than before.

"Life may shift, but I bend, not break. I adjust, I grow, I thrive."

"Change is not my enemy; it's my teacher. I embrace it and become stronger."

"No matter what life brings, I have the courage and flexibility to keep moving forward."

"I flow with life's changes, turning challenges into opportunities for growth."

"Even when the path changes, my determination and resilience guide me onward."

Steve Jobs, the co-founder of Apple, was famously **fired from his own company** in 1985. Many would have seen it as the end, but he adapted. He founded **NeXT** and **Pixar**, learning and growing through those experiences. Eventually, he returned to Apple, leading it to create revolutionary products like the iPhone and iPad.

His story shows that even after major setbacks or life changes, adapting, learning, and staying persistent can turn what seems like failure into incredible success.

Turn the page on every 'if' that held you captive. Beyond the shadows of regret lies your brilliance, your resilience, your freedom. Live it. Own it. Shine."

"The 'ifs' will always linger, tempting us with what might have been, but they do not define us. Beyond every hesitation, every doubt, every regret, there is a life waiting to be claimed—full of purpose, courage, and possibility. Your strength has carried you this far, and it will carry you farther. Step boldly into your tomorrow, for it is yours to shape, yours to live, and yours to love. Life beyond 'if' is not a dream—it is your power in motion."

No more 'ifs.' No more waiting. Beyond doubt, beyond fear, beyond every shadow that once held you back, there is only forward—only growth, only courage, only life fully lived. You are stronger than your hesitations, braver than your fears, and the author of every moment yet to come.

Step into it. Own it. Shine. This is life beyond 'if'—and it is yours."

"Best of luck in your life and with all the 'ifs......' I don't know if our journey together was good or bad, but it would make me truly happy if, as my companion on this path, you've learned something that you'll carry into your life. Thank you for sharing this journey with me. Remember, I am always here for you—so don't worry. Thank you, my dear, lovable companion."

"With gratitude, hope, and belief in your strength—go live your life beyond 'if'."

The Mirror Within: Facing Your True Self

- What is the one "If" that has been holding you back from taking action for the last year?

- If the fear of failure were completely removed from your life today, what would be the very first thing you would do?

- Are you waiting for the "perfect moment," or are you waiting for permission? Who are you waiting for that permission from?

7-Day "What If" Challenge Workbook

Turn your "what if" worries into action and confidence.

Day 1: Awareness

Morning:

Write 3 "what if" thoughts:

1. ------------

2. ------------

3. -----------

Evening

One action I can take tomorrow: _________

Day 2: Reframe

Morning:

Pick 1 fear: _________

If it happens, I can: _________

What I can learn: _________

Evening:

Today I noticed fear but stayed calm when: _________

Day 3: Control

Morning

Worry _________

I can control _________

I cannot control: _________

Evening:

One small action I took: _________

Day 4: Action

Morning:

One small step I will take today:

Evening:

What I did: _________

How it felt: __________

What I learned: ___________

Day 5: Past Wins

Morning:

A past fear I faced: _________

What I did well: _________

Lesson I learned: _________

Evening:

One way I can use this today: _________

Day 6: Mindfulness

Morning:

Minutes of mindfulness: _________

When a “what if” appeared, I: _________

Evening:

How it helped me today: _________

Day 7: Celebrate

Morning:

Remaining fears: _________

Action I can take: _________

What I can let go: _________

Evening:

3 wins this week:

1. ---------------

2. --------------

3. --------------

Tip: Repeat each week. Little steps every day turn "what if" worries into courage and action

We'd love to hear how it went for you. Share your experience, insights, or favorite moments

On Instagram and tag us: **@mindlift_with_vaibhav**.

About the author

Vaibhav Srivastav is an educator, psychologist, Archaeologist and author dedicated to empowering individuals through mental clarity and personal growth. With a professional background in national institutes coordination and behavioral science, he brings a unique, practical perspective to the world of self-help.

As a deep believer in the power of mindset, Vaibhav is the founder of platforms like *Mindlift*, where he shares insights on motivation and life management. His writing aims to bridge the gap between psychological principles and everyday challenges. **Life Beyond If** is his latest contribution to helping readers move past hesitation and toward a life of purpose

www.ingramcontent.com/pod-product-compliance
Lightning Source LLC
Chambersburg PA
CBHW050019170726
48282CB00025B/462